The Music Man's Songbook

by Jon Lawrence
Illustrated by Gemma Wells

Dear Lacey
I hope you enjoy
singing these songs
at home!
the Music Man

First published in 2017 by
Bird's Nest Books
www.birdsnestbooks.co.uk

ISBN 978-0-9932614-5-9

About the book

These songs have been performed to hundreds of children over the last two years. They are open to many physical actions and child participation. However, they are designed to help children understand sounds and numbers and to encourage movement. Above all, they are to be enjoyed.

The Music Man's Songbook

Five Little Caterpillars

Five little caterpillars munching on a leaf,
MUNCH! MUNCH! MUNCH!
Then one became a butterfly,
Fluttered low and fluttered high,
And flew away free.

Four little caterpillars munching on a leaf
MUNCH! MUNCH! MUNCH!
Then one became a butterfly,
Fluttered low and fluttered high,
And flew away free.

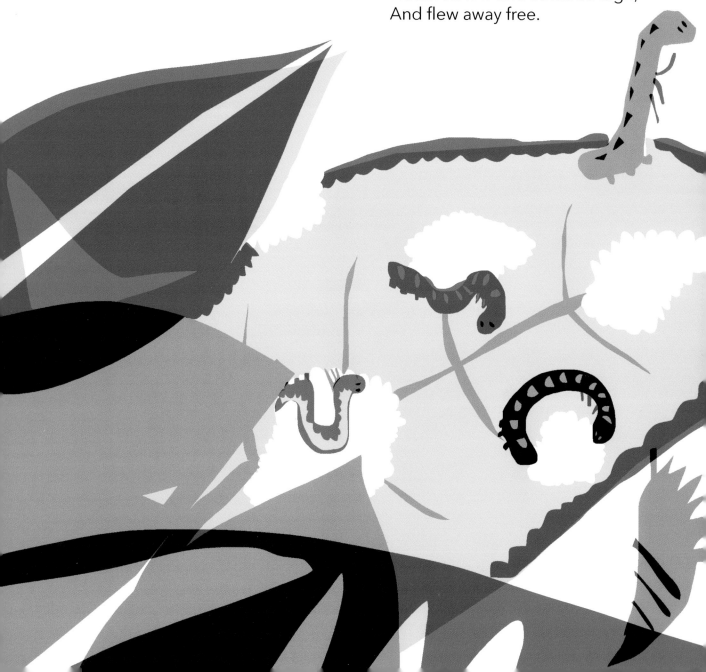

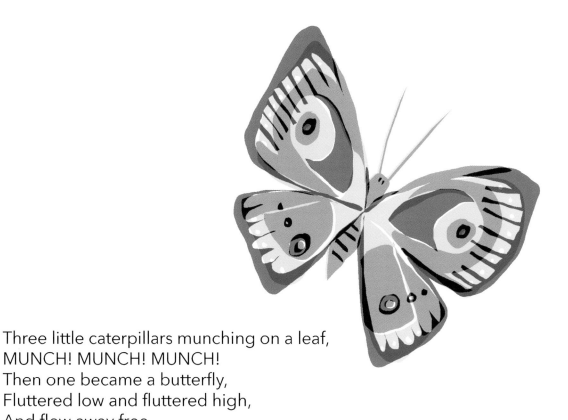

Three little caterpillars munching on a leaf,
MUNCH! MUNCH! MUNCH!
Then one became a butterfly,
Fluttered low and fluttered high,
And flew away free.

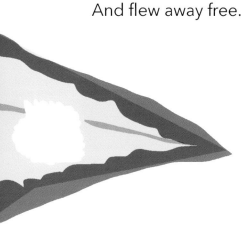

Two little caterpillars munching on a leaf,
MUNCH! MUNCH! MUNCH!
Then one became a butterfly,
Fluttered low and fluttered high,
And flew away free.

One little caterpillar munching on a leaf,
MUNCH! MUNCH! MUNCH!
Then one became a butterfly,
Fluttered low and fluttered high,
And flew away free.

The Body Song

I have a body,
It's not too shoddy,
There are lots of things I can do.
I can blink my eyes,
I can slap my thighs,
I have a wonderful body I can use.

I have a body,
It's not too shoddy,
There are lots of things I can do.
I can wiggle my toes,
I can twitch my nose,
I have a wonderful body I can use.

I have a body,
It's not too shoddy,
There are lots of things I can do.
I can shake my head,
Or my hands instead,
I have a wonderful body I can use.

I have a body,
It's not too shoddy,
There are lots of things I can do.
Take air in my lungs,
Or wiggle my tongue,
I have a wonderful body I can use.

I have a body,
It's not too shoddy,
There are lots of things I can do.
I can jump and hop,
I can run then stop,
I have a wonderful body I can use.

Five Little Leaves

Five little leaves on an autumn tree,
Swaying to and fro.
Then one little leaf was swept away
by the breeze,
And drifted high and low.
I wonder where did it go?
Where did it go?
I wonder where did it go?

Four little leaves on an autumn tree,
Swaying to and fro.
Then one little leaf was swept away
by the breeze,
And drifted high and low.
I wonder where did it go?
Where did it go?
I wonder where did it go?

Three little leaves on an autumn tree,
Swaying to and fro.
Then one little leaf was swept away
by the breeze,
And drifted high and low.
I wonder where did it go?
Where did it go?
I wonder where did it go?

Two little leaves on an autumn tree,
Swaying to and fro.
Then one little leaf was swept away
by the breeze,
And drifted high and low.
I wonder where did it go?
Where did it go?
I wonder where did it go?

One little leaf on an autumn tree,
Swaying to and fro.
Then one little leaf was swept away
by the breeze,
And drifted high and low.
I wonder where did it go?
Where did it go?
I wonder where did it go?

HEY!

You put your left arm up
and wave it in the air,
You put your right arm up
and wave it in the air,
You put both arms up and
wave them in the air,
And shout HEY at the top of your voice!

HEY!

You put your left leg up
and wave it in the air,
You put your right leg up
and wave it in the air,
You put both legs up
and wave them in the air,
And shout HEY at the top of your voice!

HEY!

You raise your hands and legs
and wave them in the air,
You raise your hands and legs
and wave them in the air,
You raise your hands and legs
and wave them in the air,
And shout HEY at the top of your voice!

HEY!

You put your whole self up
and wave it in the air,
You put your whole self up
and wave it in the air,
You put your whole self up and
wave it in the air,
And shout HEY at the top of your voice!

HEY!

And shout HEY at the top of your voice!

HEY!

And shout HEY at the top of your voice!

HEY!

Pull a Funny Face

Do you know what makes me happy?
Do you know what makes me smile?
It's to pull a funny face every once in a while.
You can pull a funny face,
Pull a funny face,
Pull a funny face,
Every once in a while.

When I'm feeling lonely,
When I'm feeling blue,
I pull myself together,
And this is what I do.
I just pull a funny face,
Pull a funny face,
Pull a funny face,
Every once in a while.

When the rain is falling,
When the skies are grey,
There's something you can do
To brighten up your day.
You can pull a funny face,
Pull a funny face,
Pull a funny face,
Every once in a while.

Dippy the Diplodocus

I'm a diplodocus long and fat,
I eat my leaves but that is that.
If you try to catch me,
I'll swat you with my tail,
SPLAT!

Because I'm a diplodocus,
And that is that.

How do you get around?

I once met a snake while walking one day,
He smiled at what
I had to say.
I said, "Snake, how do you get around?"
He said, "Easy! I slither on the ground."

He went slither, slither, slither on the ground,
He went slither, slither, slither all around,
He went slither, slither here and slither, slither there,
"That's how I get around."

I once met a rabbit while walking one day,
He smiled at what
I had to say.
I said, "Rabbit, how do you get around?"
He said, "Easy! I hop along the ground."

He went hop, hop,
hop on the ground,
He went hop, hop, hop all
around,
He went hop, hop here
and hop, hop there,
"That's how I get around."

I once met a bird while
walking one day,
He smiled at what
I had to say.
I said, "Bird, how do
you get around?"
He said, "Easy! I fly above
the ground."

He went flip, flap,
fly above the ground,
He went flip, flap,
fly all around,
He went flip, flap here
and flip, flap there,
"That's how I get around."

The Weather Song

What kind of weather will we have today?
What kind of weather will we have today?
Can we go outside and play?
What kind of weather will we have today?

We might have rain,
Falling, falling, falling down,
We might have rain,
Falling, falling, falling down,
But we can jump in the puddles
with a splish, splosh, splash,
We might even hear a thunder crash.

What kind of weather will we have today?
What kind of weather will we have today?
Can we go outside and play?
What kind of weather will we have today?

We might have wind,
Blowing, blowing, blowing round,
We might have wind,
Blowing, blowing, blowing round,
A gale may blow with all its might,
We could go out and fly a kite.

What kind of weather will we have today?
What kind of weather will we have today?
Can we go outside and play?
What kind of weather will we have today?

We might have snow,
Freezing, freezing, freezing cold,
We might have snow,
Freezing, freezing, freezing cold,
We could build a snowman
with a hat and scarf,
With a funny smile to make us all laugh.

What kind of weather will we have today?
What kind of weather will we have today?
Can we go outside and play?
What kind of weather will we have today?

We might have sun,
Shining, shining, shining bright,
We might have sun,
Shining, shining, shining bright,
We might need to cool off in the sea,
Or walk the beach with a nice ice-cream.

What kind of weather will we have today?
What kind of weather will we have today?
Can we go outside and play?
What kind of weather will we have today?

Dozy Daisy Donkey

Dozy Daisy Donkey in the summer heat,
Saw Curly Katy Kitty-Cat trip over her feet.
Dozy Daisy Donkey said, "What a silly cat!
She-awwlways, she-awwlways, she-awwlways
She always does that."

Dozy Daisy Donkey beneath the summer sky,
Saw Buzby the Bumblebee busily buzzing by.
He flew into a tree with a great big SPLAT!
And Dozy Daisy Donkey said,
"He-awwlways, he-awwlways, he-awwlways
He always does that."

Dozy Daisy Donkey lazing lazily,
Saw Squiry the Squirley Squirrel fall out of his tree.
He landed on his head with a rattle-tat-tat
And Dozy Daisy Donkey said,
"He-awwlways, he-awwlways, he-awwlways
He always does that."

Jack-in-the-Box

There's a Jack-in-the-Box opening an eye,
There's a Jack-in-the-Box wriggling inside,
But if you count with me, one, two, three,
You can set the Jack-in-the-Box free.
One! Two! Three!

There's a Jack-in-the-Box jumping up and down,
There's a Jack-in-the-Box spinning around,
From left to right, front to back,
He is a jolly, jolly jumping Jack.

There's a Jack-in-the-Box coiled up tight,
There's a Jack-in-the-Box, he'll give you such a fright,
But if you count with me, one, two, three,
You can set the Jack-in-the-Box free.
One! Two! Three!

There's a Jack-in-the-Box jumping up and down,
There's a Jack-in-the-Box spinning around,
From left to right, front to back,
He is a jolly, jolly jumping Jack.

There's a Jack-in-the-Box with a lid on top,
There's a Jack-in-the-Box getting ready to pop!
But if you count with me, one, two, three,
You can set the Jack-in-the-Box free.
One! Two! Three!

There's a Jack-in-the-Box jumping up and down,
There's a Jack-in-the-Box spinning around,
From left to right, front to back,
He is a jolly, jolly jumping Jack.

Keep Fit

You've got to keep fit,
You've got to keep fit,
You've got a real cool body
But you've got to take care of it.
Reach up high
And touch the sky.
You've got to keep fit,
You've got to keep fit.

You've got to keep fit,
You've got to keep fit,
You've got a real cool body
But you've got to take care of it.
Reach down low
And touch your toes.
You've got to keep fit,
You've got to keep fit.

You've got to keep fit,
You've got to keep fit,
You've got a real cool body
But you've got to take care of it.
Why not hop
And just don't stop?
You've got to keep fit,
You've got to keep fit.

You've got to keep fit,
You've got to keep fit,
You've got a real cool body
But you've got to take care of it.
Why not run
Until the day is done?
You've got to keep fit,
You've got to keep fit.

Sleepy Koala

Sleepy Koala, Sleepy Koala
Sleeping in the tree.
You girls and boys must make no noise
Or Sleepy might fall on me… OW!
Or Sleepy might fall on me… OW!

Sleepy Koala, Sleepy Koala
Sleeps the whole day through.
You girls and boys must make no noise
Or Sleepy might fall on you… OW!
Or Sleepy might fall on you… OW!

Sleepy Koala, Sleepy Koala
Never makes a fuss.
You girls and boys must make no noise
Or Sleepy might fall on us… OW!
Or Sleepy might fall on us… OW!

About the author

Jon Lawrence is an author and musician from South Wales. Following his degree in music from the University of Leeds and his subsequent master's degree from Sheffield University, he now works in pre-schools around Norfolk, Cambridgeshire and Lincolnshire where the children know him simply as *The Music Man*. Jon has published three novels, two novellas, a full length play and a collection of school plays. As a musician he has released a number of albums in an array of genres as a solo artist and with various bands.

About the illustrator

Gemma Wells is an illustrator and writer from the Chiltern Hills who is now based in the flat Fens. Torn between her passion for the natural world and her love of creating things, she eventually decided to read Ecology at Durham University and has since had a varied career in nature conservation that has taken her to islands, forests and the other side of the world. Now the balance is restored as she is currently studying a master's degree in Children's Book Illustration alongside her wildlife work.

bonus
track